CANADIAN ICON

THE GORDON LIGHTFOOT STORY

LORI G. BROWN

All rights reserved. No part of this publication may be reproduced, distributed, or transmitted in any form or by any means, including photocopying, recording, or other electronic or mechanical methods, without the prior written permission of the publisher, except in the case of brief quotations embodied in critical reviews and certain other noncommercial uses permitted by copyright law.

Copyright © Lori G. Brown 2023.

TABLE OF CONTENTS.

CHAPTER 1

WHO IS GORDON LIGHTFOOT?
EARLY LIFE
SONGWRITING
MUSICAL CAREER.
ACCOLADES.
PERSONAL LIFE.
LIGHTFOOT'S SOUND.
DISCOGRAPHY

CHAPTER TWO

TIPS ON BECOMING A SUCCESSFUL ARTIST IN THE MUSIC INDUSTRY.

CHAPTER 1

WHO IS GORDON LIGHTFOOT?

Gordon Lightfoot is a Canadian singer-songwriter who has been active in the music industry for over six decades. He was born on November 17, 1938, in Orillia, Ontario, Canada, and began his career in the early 1960s. He was worth $40 million as at his time of death, and was 1.83m tall.

Lightfoot is known for his distinctive baritone voice and his poetic lyrics, which often explore themes of love, loss, and the natural world. Some of his most famous songs include "If You Could Read My Mind," "Sundown," "The Wreck of the Edmund Fitzgerald," and "Canadian Railroad Trilogy."

Throughout his career, Lightfoot has been recognized for his contributions to Canadian music and culture. He has received numerous awards, including 16 Juno Awards (Canada's equivalent of the Grammy Awards), and has been inducted into the Canadian Music Hall of

Fame, the Canadian Songwriters Hall of Fame, and the Order of Canada.

DATE AND PLACE OF BIRTH AND DEATH.
He was born on November 17, 1938 in Orillia, Ontario, Canada and died a natural death at Sunnybrook Health Sciences Centre in Toronto on May 1, 2023, at the age of 84.

EARLY LIFE

Gordon Lightfoot was born on November 17, 1938, in Orillia, Ontario, Canada. He was the second child of Jessie Vick Trill Lightfoot and Gordon Lightfoot Sr. Both of his parents were musically inclined, and they passed on their love of music to their son.

Lightfoot grew up in a working-class family, and his father worked as a grocer while his mother stayed at home to take care of the children. Despite the family's modest means, they were able to provide Lightfoot with piano lessons, which he began taking at the age of four.

As a child, Lightfoot was an avid reader and had a particular interest in poetry. He was also drawn to music, and he would often listen to his father playing the mandolin and piano. Lightfoot's mother was a member of the church choir, and she would often sing hymns at home.

In his teenage years, Lightfoot became interested in playing the guitar and writing his own songs. He would often perform at local coffeehouses and folk clubs, and he quickly gained a reputation as a talented songwriter and performer.

After completing high school, Lightfoot moved to Toronto to pursue a career in music. He played in a number of bands and worked as a songwriter for other artists. In 1962, he released his debut album, "Lightfoot!", which included the hit single "Remember Me (I'm the One)." The album received critical acclaim and established Lightfoot as a major talent in the Canadian music scene.

Over the next few years, Lightfoot continued to release successful albums and singles, including "Early Morning Rain" and "The Way I Feel." He became known for his poetic lyrics, intricate guitar playing, and distinctive voice, and he quickly became one of the most respected and influential songwriters of his generation.

Despite his success, Lightfoot remained grounded and focused on his music. He continued to tour and record throughout the 1960s and 1970s, and his music continued to resonate with audiences around the world.

In conclusion, Gordon Lightfoot's early life was marked by his love of music and his passion for songwriting. He grew up in a musical family and was encouraged to pursue his passion from a young age. His talent and dedication to his craft would eventually make him one of the most celebrated musicians in Canadian music history.

SONGWRITING

Lightfoot's songwriting process typically begins with a guitar melody or chord progression. He often writes songs in the key of D, which he has said is his favorite key to play in. Once he has a melody or chord progression that he likes, he will begin to work on the lyrics.

Lightfoot's lyrics are often inspired by his personal experiences and the world around him. Many of his songs are about love, relationships, and the beauty of nature. He has said that he is also inspired by history and current events, and some of his songs, such as "The Wreck of the Edmund Fitzgerald," are based on real-life events.

In terms of his writing style, Lightfoot is known for his use of vivid imagery and storytelling. He often uses metaphors and symbolism to convey his messages, and his lyrics are often open to interpretation. He has said that he wants his listeners to be able to relate to his songs in their own way and to be able to make their own connections.

Another hallmark of Lightfoot's songwriting is his intricate guitar work. He is known for his fingerpicking style, which he learned from artists like Pete Seeger and Bob Dylan. His guitar parts often complement his lyrics, adding depth and emotion to his songs.

Once Lightfoot has written a song, he will typically record a demo of it on his home studio setup. He has said that he prefers to record his demos on a 4-track tape machine, as he feels it gives his recordings a warm, analog sound. He will then bring the demo to his band to work out the arrangements and record the final version in the studio.

Overall, Gordon Lightfoot's songwriting is characterized by his ability to tell compelling stories through his lyrics and his intricate guitar melodies. His songs are often inspired by his personal experiences and the world around him, and he has a talent for using vivid imagery and storytelling to convey his messages. His music has stood the test of time and continues to inspire new generations of songwriters.

MUSICAL CAREER.

Gordon Lightfoot is a Canadian singer-songwriter who has been widely regarded as one of the most important and influential figures in the country-folk music genre. Throughout his career, he has released numerous albums and has won many awards for his music. In this book, we will take a detailed look at the career life of Gordon Lightfoot.

Gordon Lightfoot was born on November 17, 1938, in Orillia, Ontario, Canada. He began playing the guitar at a young age and was heavily influenced by the folk music of artists such as Pete Seeger, Bob Dylan, and

The Weavers. He began writing his own songs and playing in coffeehouses while attending high school.

In the early 1960s, Lightfoot moved to Toronto to pursue a music career. He quickly gained a following in the city's folk music scene and was signed to United Artists Records in 1964. His debut album, "Lightfoot!", was released in 1966 and included the hit single "Early Morning Rain." The album was a critical and commercial success and established Lightfoot as a rising star in the folk music world.

RISE TO FAME.
In the late 1960s and early 1970s, Lightfoot continued to release successful albums and singles. He had several hits on the Billboard charts, including "If You Could Read My Mind," "Carefree Highway," and "Sundown." He also won several Juno Awards, which are the Canadian equivalent of the Grammy Awards.

Lightfoot's music was known for its poetic lyrics and storytelling, and he often drew inspiration from the

Canadian landscape and his own personal experiences. He was also known for his distinctive baritone voice and finger-picking guitar style.

In 1976, Lightfoot released his most famous album, "Summertime Dream," which included the hit single "The Wreck of the Edmund Fitzgerald." The song, which tells the story of the sinking of a Great Lakes freighter, was a massive hit and reached No. 2 on the Billboard Hot 100 chart. It has since become one of Lightfoot's signature songs and is considered a classic of the folk-rock genre.

LATER CAREER AND LEGACY.
Throughout the 1980s and 1990s, Lightfoot continued to release albums and tour extensively. He had several more hits, including "The Circle Is Small," "Stay Loose," and "Restless." He also continued to win awards and accolades, including induction into the Canadian Music Hall of Fame in 1986 and the Order of Canada in 1987.

In the 2000s, Lightfoot experienced some health issues but continued to perform and record music. He released his final album, "Solo," in 2004, which featured stripped-down versions of some of his most famous songs. In 2012, he suffered a stroke but made a full recovery and returned to touring in 2013.

Lightfoot's influence on the folk music genre and Canadian music as a whole has been significant. He has been called "Canada's greatest songwriter" by some critics and has inspired countless musicians with his poetic lyrics and unique sound. Many artists have covered his songs, including Elvis Presley, Johnny Cash, and Bob Dylan.

In mid-April 2023, Lightfoot's declining health caused him to cancel the remainder of his 2023 tour. He then died of natural causes in Sunnybrook hospital, Canada. Gordon Lightfoot is a Canadian music icon whose career has spanned more than five decades. He has released numerous albums and has won many awards for his music. His storytelling and poetic lyrics have made him one of the most influential figures in the folk music genre, and his legacy continues to inspire new generations of musicians.

ACCOLADES.

Gordon Lightfoot is a Canadian singer-songwriter and guitarist who has received numerous honors and awards throughout his long and successful career. Below is a detailed rundown of some of his most notable accolades:

1. Canadian Music Hall of Fame:
In 1986, Lightfoot was inducted into the Canadian Music Hall of Fame in recognition of his contribution to Canadian music.

2. Juno Awards:
Lightfoot has won a total of 16 Juno Awards over the course of his career, including "Folk Singer of the Year" in 1966 and "Male Vocalist of the Year" in 1975.

3. Canadian Country Music Hall of Fame:
In 2001, Lightfoot was inducted into the Canadian Country Music Hall of Fame.

4. Canadian Songwriters Hall of Fame:
In 2003, Lightfoot was inducted into the Canadian Songwriters Hall of Fame in recognition of his contribution to Canadian music.

5. Lifetime Achievement Awards:
Lightfoot has received several lifetime achievement awards, including the Governor General's Performing Arts Award for Lifetime Artistic Achievement in 1997 and the SOCAN Lifetime Achievement Award in 2015.

6. Walk of Fame:
In 1998, Lightfoot was awarded a star on Canada's Walk of Fame in recognition of his contribution to Canadian music.

7. International recognition:
Lightfoot has also been recognized internationally, receiving a Grammy nomination for "Best Folk Album" in 1971 and induction into the Songwriters Hall of Fame in 2012.

8. Queen Elizabeth II Diamond Jubilee Medal:
In 2012, Lightfoot was awarded the Queen Elizabeth II Diamond Jubilee Medal in recognition of his contributions to Canadian culture and music.

9. Honorary Doctorates:
Lightfoot has received several honorary doctorates from universities in Canada, including Lakehead University, Laurentian University, and the University of Toronto.

10. Allan Waters Humanitarian Award:
In 2003, Lightfoot was presented with the Allan Waters Humanitarian Award at the Juno Awards in

recognition of his charitable work and contributions to humanitarian causes.

11. Canada's Walk of Fame Peter Soumalias Award:
In 2018, Lightfoot received the Canada's Walk of Fame Peter Soumalias Award in recognition of his positive impact on the music industry in Canada.

The 2019 documentary "Gordon Lightfoot: If You Could Read My Mind" focused on his life and career. In 2022, Lightfoot was honored with the Golden Plate Award from the American Academy of Achievement. Lightfoot's contributions to Canadian music and culture have been significant, and he has been recognized with numerous accolades throughout his career.

PERSONAL LIFE.

Gordon Lightfoot is a Canadian singer-songwriter who rose to fame in the 1960s and 1970s with hits such as "If

You Could Read My Mind," "Sundown," and "The Wreck of the Edmund Fitzgerald." Lightfoot has a private personal life, but some information is publicly available.

Lightfoot was born on November 17, 1938, in Orillia, Ontario, Canada. His parents were Jessie Vick Trill Lightfoot and Gordon Lightfoot Sr. His father was a heavy equipment operator, and his mother was a housewife. Lightfoot grew up in Orillia, where he developed an interest in music from a young age. He learned to play piano and later added the guitar and drums to his repertoire.

Lightfoot was married three times in his life. His first marriage was to Margaret Anne Rich, whom he met in 1960. They married in 1963 and had two children, Fred and Ingrid. The marriage ended in 1973. Lightfoot's second marriage was to Brita Ingegerd Olaisson, whom he met in Sweden while on tour. They married in 1989 but divorced in 2011. Lightfoot's third marriage was to Kim Hasse, whom he married in 2014.

In addition to his marriages, Lightfoot had a long-term relationship with Cathy Smith, who was a backup singer and drug dealer. Smith was involved in the death of John Belushi, for which she served time in prison. Lightfoot wrote a song about Smith called "Sundown," which was a hit in 1974.

Lightfoot has been open about his struggles with alcoholism and has been sober since the late 1980s. He suffered a serious abdominal hemorrhage in 2002 and was hospitalized for several weeks. He has since recovered but has cut back on his touring schedule.

Lightfoot has received numerous awards and accolades throughout his career, including induction into the Canadian Music Hall of Fame, the Canadian Country Music Hall of Fame, and the Songwriters Hall of Fame. He continues to perform and record music, with his most recent album, "Solo," released in 2020.

Aside from his personal life, Lightfoot has been known to be an avid sports fan, particularly in hockey and baseball. He was a minor league baseball player before pursuing his music career and has also played in several charity hockey games. He is also a supporter of the Toronto Blue Jays baseball team.

Lightfoot has had a successful career in music, with over 20 studio albums and numerous hits. His music is known for its storytelling, often focusing on Canadian history and culture. His song "The Wreck of the Edmund Fitzgerald" is one of his most famous and tells the story of the sinking of the freighter in Lake Superior. Many of his other songs have become classics, including "Early Morning Rain," "Carefree Highway," and "Rainy Day People."

In addition to his music, Lightfoot has also dabbled in acting. He appeared in the film "Harry Tracy, Desperado" in 1982 and had a cameo in the television series "Due South" in 1997. He also appeared in an episode of the Canadian television series "Corner Gas" in 2005.

Throughout his career, Lightfoot has maintained his privacy and kept his personal life out of the public eye. He has been described as a private person who prefers to let his music speak for itself. Despite this, he has remained a beloved figure in Canadian music and continues to inspire new generations of musicians.

LIGHTFOOT'S SOUND.

Gordon Lightfoot's sound is often described as a blend of folk, country, and pop, with a focus on his acoustic guitar playing and storytelling lyrics. He has been compared to other folk singers such as Bob Dylan, but his sound is unique and distinctive.

Lightfoot's songs are characterized by his rich baritone voice, which is often accompanied by acoustic guitar, piano, and other traditional instruments such as mandolin, harmonica, and fiddle. His guitar playing is intricate and melodic, often featuring fingerpicking and alternating bass patterns. His melodies are memorable and singable, with catchy hooks and memorable choruses.

Lyrically, Lightfoot's songs often tell stories of everyday people and events, as well as Canadian history and culture. His lyrics are poetic and often introspective, with a focus on personal reflection and the human experience. He has been praised for his ability to capture the essence of a place or a moment in time with his words, making his songs both universal and specific.

One of Lightfoot's most distinctive elements is his use of vocal harmony, often featuring layered backing vocals that add depth and texture to his songs. This is particularly evident on songs such as "If You Could Read My Mind," "Carefree Highway," and "Rainy Day People."

While Lightfoot's sound has evolved over the years, he has remained true to his folk and country roots. His music has influenced countless artists in Canada and around the world, and his legacy continues to inspire new generations of musicians.

DISCOGRAPHY

Gordon Lightfoot is a Canadian singer-songwriter and guitarist who has been active in the music industry since the 1960s. He has released numerous albums throughout his career, some of which are listed below:

- Lightfoot! (1966)
- The Way I Feel (1967)
- Did She Mention My Name? (1968)
- Back Here on Earth (1968)
- Sunday Concert (1969)
- Sit Down Young Stranger (1970)
- Summer Side of Life (1971)

- Don Quixote (1972)
- Old Dan's Records (1972)
- Sundown (1974)
- Cold on the Shoulder (1975)
- Summertime Dream (1976)
- Endless Wire (1978)
- Dream Street Rose (1980)
- Shadows (1982)
- Salute (1983)
- East of Midnight (1986)
- Waiting for You (1993)
- A Painter Passing Through (1998)
- Harmony (2004)
- Solo (2020)

In addition to these studio albums, Lightfoot has also released several live albums, compilations, and singles throughout his career. Some of his most popular songs include "If You Could Read My Mind," "The Wreck of the Edmund Fitzgerald," "Sundown".

CHAPTER TWO

TIPS ON BECOMING A SUCCESSFUL ARTIST IN THE MUSIC INDUSTRY.

A successful musical career does not develop overnight. I wrote about this in one of my other books, however ,we will go through them again in this book. To clearly define your objectives and make them a reality, requires time, persistence, being open to criticism, and even some failure.

Here are some crucial methods to think about as you lay the groundwork for long-term success in the music business.

1. Remain current
The music business is always evolving. You must be informed if you want to keep up. Both musicians and anyone working in the music industry should be aware of this. You must be able to discuss the trends driving the industry's expansion if you want to work in licensing, product design, or marketing at a company

like Spotify or Apple. Similarly to this, an effective artist manager should be knowledgeable about market preferences and trends, developing niche markets, and shifting opinions on an artist's financial viability.

The bulk of well-known top executives and artists did not travel a straight or narrow route to success. Your route will need constant learning, grit, and investment in yourself, just as theirs did.

The way that music is distributed has drastically altered in recent years, so signing a contract with a big label is no longer necessary for musicians to be successful. It will be easier to market your music and get a large audience if you keep up with the latest developments on websites like SoundCloud, YouTube, Instagram, and Facebook's Sound Collection.

2. Network with others in the field.
To advance your career and build a personal brand in the music business, you must develop and keep up mutually beneficial partnerships.

"Networking and innovative partnerships are important," you often hear. Why? Like every other sector that depends on the human race, the music business benefits from it. So where do you even begin?

Take frequent breaks from the studio, your keyboard, or your microphone to engage in face-to-face conversations with peers, coworkers, and seasoned experts. You have other options for networking besides industry conferences, trade exhibitions, and festivals, which provide ideal venues for enjoyable and natural conversations. Networking is now simpler than ever thanks to social media platforms like Facebook, LinkedIn, and Instagram. Create a profile on these or other sites if you haven't already, and then start interacting with others. Whether you are creating new contacts in person or online, be intentionally persistent. Note anyone you meet and any reasons why you two would profit from continuing to communicate.

3. Keep your spirits up at all times.

Your ability to manipulate it makes it the only actual survival tool you have. You will be more resilient to the neglect you may experience when initially starting if you approach things with unwavering positivity.

You'll see how well I know this! Keep in mind that the entry barrier into the music industry is quite high, so try not to take things personally.

Every year, some 80,000 albums are issued, and Billboard and other related rankings provide information on a rotating Top 200. That amounts to 0.25 percent of all releases each year which is noteworthy enough to be noticed.

4. Study Excellence and Excel in Your Field

This is true for whatever you do! Your musical tastes set the tone for everything. Sometimes society may teach us to have lower standards by persuading us that mediocrity is okay. Not at all. Excellence is available to you; all you need to do is understand and practice it.

Pay close attention to your music instructors if they are knowledgeable in both music theory and enjoyment. Learn from others who have achieved success in the music industry.

Listen to everything, regardless of the genre, and make an effort to find the beauty in every music, regardless of your particular tastes.

Your music career will be shaped by the foundation you create today with your acceptance and comprehension of these fundamental concepts.

5. Invest in your future by taking on internships and on-campus jobs.

Experience is something that the music business values highly. How does one get experience?

Internships and on-campus employment are two methods to impress future employers. Internships are a very beneficial way to explore potential career paths, hone job-related skills, and acquire knowledge of how professionals in the field live and operate. They let you temporarily migrate to bustling cities like Beijing and London, as well as to domestic hotspots like Los Angeles, New York City, and Nashville. Internships are widely used by employers as hiring trials. To avoid losing out on potential talent, they are fast to provide a job offer if they are impressed.

You have several possibilities and options for acquiring useful experience. The only two things that will impress and appeal to companies are internships and student employment.

6. Recognize your competitive edge.
You have a long array of abilities. Consider your background and the things that set you apart from other people. You'll need a well-constructed elevator pitch that introduces you to the audience and specifically highlights your unique set of abilities, background, and presence.

You'll be a fantastic improviser as a musician and artist, always ready to present a song you've been creating or grab your guitar and go onstage to cover for a buddy at a show. Additionally, you'll be well-versed in project management. You've mastered time management, comprehend the necessity for attention to detail, and appreciate the value of being both a leader and a team player, whether it's managing marketing or event logistics for an upcoming campus program or arranging and rehearsing band members for a performance.

7. Be flexible

The music and entertainment industries don't have a set path for getting from A to Z. There is no assurance that you will earn a certain wage, get a job that lasts a lifetime, or strike a deal right away. It's better to admit and accept it right away. However, there is a strong chance that your dedication to making it big in this industry will have an influence and be rewarding.

You must develop the ability to be flexible and at ease changing course as opportunities arise. In certain cases, you may even need to pursue a non-musical lifeline vocation to support yourself, your significant other, or your family. The bulk of well-known top executives and artists did not travel a straight or narrow route to success. Your route will need constant learning, grit, and investment in yourself, just as theirs did.

8. Create a solid professional peer group that serves as your sounding board.
Although family and friends are wonderful, they are sometimes too prejudiced to provide helpful suggestions and counsel on your musical endeavors.

Professionals in the music industry may establish more reasonable expectations and can often provide more useful advice. Don't forget that Grandma will probably approve of whatever you do, so don't take her counsel too seriously.

9. Recognize that nobody just gets up and dons their famous pants.

Success in the music industry seldom follows a straight path. There is always a tale to tell about how and when it all transpired by the time an artist enters the public eye.

Sadly, the majority of your new admirers won't get to see this stage of your adventure. To the average person, the illusion is that you got up one day, composed a song, and put on your well-known jeans. Don't allow the difficult journey to achievement to depress you; it's quite natural!

BONUS: Volunteer and mentor.
Your successors will benefit from your guidance and experience. Make an effort, give to the arts and education, mentor, and educate!

Nothing is more soul-satisfying than seeing a young kid succeed as a result of what you have taught them.

If you are successful, give to a charity that gives disadvantaged children the chance to hear music, which is a gift that is greater than themselves.

That's all there is to it. I hope you took in some of this and may use it in your artistic endeavors. Wishing you luck and keep rocking!

Made in United States
North Haven, CT
05 January 2025